The Electric Skateboard Revolution

Tips, Tech, and Buying Guides

Table of Contents

Chapter 1. Introduction

Special Report: "The Electric Skateboard Revolution: Tips, Tech, and Buying Guides" brings forth a thrilling blend of practical advice, innovative technology, and comprehensive buying guides for skateboard enthusiasts, tech hobbyists, and transportation trend-watchers alike! Feel the rush of breeze as you cruise through cutting-edge e-skate technologies that are revolutionizing urban commutes, embrace the freedom of effortlessly gliding over city streets, or simply bask in the joy of a new exhilarating hobby. Perfectly suited for both newcomers and seasoned riders, this report demystifies technical jargon and offers clear, concise tips in a manageable platform. You'll find everything you need to confidently make your first electric skateboard purchase or upgrade your current ride, while exploring the exciting world of movement electrification. Strap in for an engaging journey that promises to revolutionize your perspective on modern personal transit!

Chapter 2. The Rise of the Electric Skateboard: A Brief History

To fully comprehend the soaring popularity of electric skateboards, it's essential to first understand the origin and evolution of this revolutionary technology. The fascination with personal mobility devices dates back to the 1950s. Skateboards - unpowered back then - started as simple wooden boards with roller-skate wheels attached, primarily used by surfers to practice when waves were low. As skateboarding began to gain momentum in the 1960s and 1970s, technological innovations and design modifications steadily improved the board's functionality, transforming it into a prominent symbol of youth culture.

Fast forward to the late 1990s, and a Californian named Louie Finkle (also known as Electric Louie) hit upon a novel idea that fused the agility of skateboards with the power of electronic devices, setting the prodigious stage for the advent of motorized skateboards. He swiftly patented his invention - marking a significant milestone in the annals of skateboard history.

2.1. Early Electric Skateboards

Finkle's first electric skateboard models were bulky and weighed close to 100 pounds. They had lead-acid batteries, brushed motors, belt-drives and basic handheld remote controls. Despite having a short 3-mile range and a sluggish top speed of 10 mph, these early electric skateboards captured the public's imagination.

Lower manufacturing costs, widespread societal acceptance, and the thrill of powered coasting drove its initial success. Electric skateboards seamlessly melded utility with an element of fun, presenting a compelling alternative to traditional skateboards. However, issues concerning the weight, limited battery life, and comparably underpowered performance compared to today's models hindered wider adoption.

2.2. Technological Evolution

Technological advances in the 2000s imparted substantial momentum to the electric skateboard evolution. The substitution of lead-acid batteries with lighter lithium-ion batteries significantly reduced the board's overall weight, facilitating increased portability. Incorporation of brushless motors, instead of brushed counterparts, enhanced efficiency, durability, and extended the board's lifespan. Developments in wireless technology enabled more precise control over speed and braking.

Advancements in wheel designs improved ride quality considerably. Soft, large-diameter polyurethane wheels began replacing hard plastic wheels, catering to better shock absorption, grip, and all-terrain capabilities. Most importantly, these advancements. catapulted electric skateboard performance to new heights - invigorating ride experience, extending travel range, and augmenting overall speed.

2.3. Mass Market Adoption and Today's Electric Skateboard Scene

Mass adoption of electric skateboards kicked off around 2012, largely triggered by Boosted Boards' landmark crowd-funding campaign. Innovations in technology, coupled with strategic marketing, positioned the electric skateboard as a legitimate commuting option, aspiring beyond a mere recreational pursuit.

Today, the global electric skateboard market is experiencing a boom.

As urban areas seek greener and more efficient modes of transportation, electric skateboards fit the bill perfectly. Portable, environmentally-friendly, and immensely enjoyable—they offer a unique solution to short-distance travel and last-mile commute problems.

The market is teeming with a plethora of designs and models to cater to various consumer needs, from lightweight, compact boards tailored for commuters to high-speed, all-terrain models for adventure enthusiasts. Each subsequent generation of electric skateboards edge closer towards achieving a perfect synergy between weight, speed, range, and affordability—underlining its ever-growing popularity.

2.4. Looking Ahead: The Future of Electric Skateboards

The electric skateboard industry's trajectory appears promising, with emerging technologies paving the way for safer, more durable, and efficient e-skate products. One such development is the emergence of regenerative braking systems, where wasted energy when braking is funneled back into the battery, thereby augmenting the board's range.

Also, given the rising attention to safety concerns, integration of various features like LED lights for night-visibility, built-in GPS tracking, and smart braking systems can be expected in the future models. Moreover, further evolutions may lead to more lightweight designs, longer battery life, and even integration with smart city infrastructure like autonomous vehicles and IoT-empowered traffic systems.

Lastly, we can't ignore the potential implications of progressive legal recognitions, as more countries and cities are now framing laws to regulate and legalize electric skates—a testament to their increasing relevance in urban mobility.

In this ever-expanding universe of electric skateboards, their rise undeniably characterizes a seminal shift in transport dynamics. This sustainable, efficient, and fascinating mode of commute, having stirred a radical revolution, is here to stay—and continues to evolve, promising brighter horizons in the realm of personal electrified transportation.

Chapter 3. Basic Guide to Understanding Electric Skateboards

Electric skateboards are a spin-off from traditional skateboarding, but with the power to go uphill. Instead of kicking off the ground to gain speed, these boards use electric motors powered by lithium-ion batteries. They are often controlled by a wireless handheld remote or sometimes even your own body weight. This basic guide is designed to cover all you need to know about these exciting pieces of tech, from their anatomy to picking the right model for your needs.

3.1. Anatomy of an Electric Skateboard

Understanding an electric skateboard starts by familiarizing yourself with its basic components:

1. **Deck**: This is the actual board you stand on during your electrifying rides. It could be made of bamboo for flexibility or Canadian maple for sturdiness. These decks are often longer than traditional skateboards to accommodate the electronics beneath.

2. **Trucks**: The trucks are connected to the wheels and the deck, and they influence the turn and overall performance of the board.

3. **Wheels**: These are quite similar to regular skateboard wheels but come in a range of sizes. The size and hardness of the wheels can affect your ride's speed, grip, and smoothness.

4. **Motor**: The motor powers your skateboard. It's either a belt-drive motor or a hub motor, each delivering power in a distinct way.

5. **Battery**: The battery powers the electric skateboard's motor. The

battery life and charge time can considerably influence your skateboarding experience.

6. **Electronic Speed Controller (ESC)**: The ESC is essentially the brain of the skateboard, controlling how power from the battery gets to the motor based on input from the remote control.

7. **Remote control**: This handheld device allows you to control the skateboard's speed, direction, and braking.

3.2. The Motors and Drives

Electric skateboards have different types of motor systems that offer various advantages and disadvantages:

1. **Belt-drive motors** are the most common. This system has motors mounted externally and connected to the wheels by belts and pulleys. Belt-drive motors provide a lot of torque and thus excellent acceleration and hill-climbing power, but they require regular maintenance and replacements as the belts wear out.

2. **Hub motors** are housed directly inside the skateboard wheels. This type of motor offers less torque than a belt-drive motor but requires less maintenance, provides quieter rides, and offers the possibility for free-wheeling when the motor is off.

3. **Direct drive motors** are a hybrid of belt-drive and hub motors. They deliver the smooth free-rolling of hub motors and the power of belt-driven ones. They are quieter and require less maintenance than a belt-driven system.

4. **Gear drive motors** offer the benefits of both belt-drive and hub motors while eliminating many of the downsides. They provide powerful torque, allow for free-rolling, and require less regular maintenance than belt-drives.

3.3. Battery Power and Range

The battery is a crucial component of the skateboard's functionality. Most electric skateboards will use a lithium-ion battery due to its high energy density and long lifespan. The capacity of the battery, usually measured in watt-hours (Wh), greatly influences the range of your e-skateboard. A larger capacity implies a longer range but also increases the weight of the skateboard.

Battery voltage and current also affect the skateboard's top speed and acceleration. Moreover, understand the charging times. Portable chargers will charge slower but are convenient for on-the-go situations, while fast home chargers will quickly get your board ready for action.

3.4. Board and Wheel Types

There are different types of electric skateboards designed for various uses:

1. **Street boards** come with hard wheels that are perfect for smooth tarmacs, bike paths, and pavements but struggle with off-road tracks or rough surfaces.

2. **Off-road or all-terrain boards** are equipped with large, soft wheels that grip all surfaces, allowing for off-road and cross-country skateboarding.

3. **Hybrid boards** are versatile for both street and off-road uses. You can change the wheels as needed.

Note that board length and wheelbase (distance between the set of wheels) influence stability, maneuverability, and comfort. Longer boards with a wide wheelbase can be more stable but harder to turn, whereas shorter boards are easier to control but may feel less stable at high speeds.

3.5. Adjusting the Board to Suit Your Needs

Not every electric skateboard will suit every person. Therefore, consider the following personalization options:

1. **Deck flexibility**: Stiffer decks enhance stability and speed while flexible ones increase shock absorption and provide a smoother ride on rough surfaces.

2. **Adjustable trucks**: Allows for easy changing of riding styles like carving, cruising, and downhill bombing.

3. **Motor and battery configuration**: Depending on the rider's weight and daily commute, having the option to customize this can be useful for performance optimization.

4. **Wheels**: Different riding environments require different wheel properties, such as hardness, diameter, and width.

Remember that personalizing your electric skateboard might affect its warranty situation, so always verify this before making modifications.

3.6. Legalities and Safety

In many countries, the laws for skating on public roads can be quite blurry. Check your local authority's regulations on e-skateboards to avoid legal issues. Always wear safety gear, such as a helmet, knee pads, and elbow pads, irrespective of your skills and experience.

3.7. Buying Guide

When purchasing an electric skateboard, consider these key aspects:

1. Purpose: What will you use your skateboard for? The answer will

guide your choices concerning board type, battery life, and other features.

2. Budget: The price of electric skateboards can range from affordable to expensive, depending on the brand, model, components, and features.

3. Brand Reputation: Choose a reputable brand that offers warranty and after-sales service.

4. Reviews: Get insights from other riders through online reviews.

Take your time to research, compare options, and make an informed choice. Happy riding!

Chapter 4. Components of an Electric Skateboard: What Makes It Tick?

Electric skateboards, aptly termed e-skateboards, have garnered significant popularity for their blend of fun experience and practical urban mobility option. These innovative gadgets are more than just traditional skateboards with a motor attached. They are a blend of various components each playing a crucial part in offering an exciting and seamless ride.

To fully appreciate the technological symphony that unfolds every time you step on an e-skateboard, it's important to dissect the whole into its parts. So, let's deep dive into the individual components of these marvels of movement electrification.

4.1. The Deck

The deck is the part of the skateboard where the user stands while riding. A key element affecting the handling and stability of the electric skateboard, the material of the deck is pivotal for its total performance. Most e-skateboard decks are manufactured using maple, bamboo, or carbon fiber.

A deck made from maple wood is durable and rigid, providing excellent stability at high speeds. However, they are typically heavier, which might not suit lightweight or portable builds. Bamboo decks, on the other hand, are flexible and lighter, offering a more responsive and less harsh ride - an optimum choice for carving and cruising, but potentially less stable at high speeds. Lastly, carbon fiber decks are extremely lightweight and strong but come at a premium price.

The design of the deck also plays a role in providing various ride experiences. Top-mounted decks provide more leverage and deeper carves while drop-through decks lower the board's center of gravity giving it better stability and easy pushing.

4.2. The Drive System

The drive system comprises the elements that propel the skateboard. Here, we discuss the two main drive systems: belt drive and hub drive.

A belt-drive system has the motor mounted externally, connecting to the wheels via a flexible belt. This design offers greater torque, enabling superior hill-climbing performance and accelerating abilities. It also allows for easy wheel customization and typically delivers a better braking experience. However, it's more maintenance-heavy, a bit noisier, and can be less efficient than hub motors.

The hub drive system has the motor encased inside the wheel, leading to a stealthier design that often has less noise and less maintenance required. That said, the hub drive might not offer the same level of torque as belt-drives, comes with non-interchangeable wheels and might deliver a harsher ride due to less urethane on the wheel leading to less vibration absorption.

4.3. The Battery

The battery is effectively the fuel tank of the electric skateboard. Lithium-ion batteries are the most common variety used, valued for their energy density and long lifespan.

The parameters of the battery—voltage, capacity, and configuration—affect the power, endurance, and ultimately the range, speed, and recharging time of the skateboard. Therefore, a larger capacity battery will provide a longer range but increases the weight and costs. Balancing these aspects to cater to your specific needs is key.

4.4. Electronic Speed Controller (ESC)

The Electronic Speed Controller (ESC) is the brain of the electric skateboard. It manages the power output from the battery to the motor based on user input through the remote control, modulating speed and brakes.

Controllers with a smooth response to input changes offer a more pleasant and less jerky ride. Some ESCs allow for customized profiles which can change acceleration and braking curves for more personalized usage.

4.5. The Remote Control

The hand-held remote control is the rider's tool for commanding the skateboard. The design and layout of remote controls vary among different brands, but generally, they contain acceleration and braking controls and a method of communicating feedback like speed, battery level, and mode.

4.6. The Wheels

While most functionally overlooked, wheels impact ride quality, grip, and durability. Wheel size and hardness, known as "durometer," can affect ride stability and how well the skateboard handles various terrains. Larger and softer wheels roll over obstacles more easily and offer more grip, though may bring down the top speed. Smaller and harder wheels potentially yield higher speed and slide easily, but provide less grip and a harsher ride.

4.7. The Trucks

The trucks influence the handling and turn response of your electric skateboard—specifically, the ease with which you can change directions when moving. Wider trucks offer more stability at the cost of maneuverability and vice versa.

In conclusion, each component of an electric skateboard contributes significantly toward its performance and ride experience. To select the right electric skateboard, understanding these components and how they interact is essential. It empowers you to prioritize features aligning with your riding style, enabling informed decision-making while purchasing or upgrading your awesome ride. You now know what makes your electric skateboard tick!

Chapter 5. Tech Innovations: Changing the Face of Electric Skateboarding

The story of electric skateboarding is replete with progress and innovation, ranging from humble beginnings to breathtaking advancements in technology. A myriad of exciting developments are shaping the future of this electrifying personal transit form, starting with the vital components that put the 'electric' in electric skateboarding: the power system.

5.1. The Power System: Batteries and Motors

A key technological breakthrough propelling the rise of electric skateboarding has been the development of compact, powerful, and energy-efficient batteries and motors.

Today's electric skateboards most commonly use lithium-ion or lithium-polymer batteries. These light, high-capacity batteries offer impressive energy density, meaning they can store a lot of energy relative to their size. This enables electric skateboards to be compact and agile, while still providing substantial riding range.

Motor technology has seen similar jumps. The two types of motors you'll typically find in e-skateboards are Hub Motors and Belt-Driven Motors. Hub Motors are built directly into the wheels, which yields a stealthier and more streamlined design. On the contrary, Belt-Driven Motors rely on a belt-and-pulley system to drive the wheels. They're typically more powerful and offer superior torque, though they do require more maintenance than their hub counterparts.

5.2. Remote Controls and Connectivity

The advent of wireless technology has vastly improved the ease and flexibility of controlling electric skateboards. Using a handheld wireless remote control, riders can effortlessly accelerate, brake, and switch between different speed modes. Advances in Bluetooth technology have not only made these connections more reliable but also introduced smartphone integration, bringing features like firmware updates, custom riding profiles, and real-time telemetry directly to riders' fingertips.

5.3. ESC: The Brains of the Board

The Electronic Speed Controller (ESC) is an integral part of every electric skateboard. It's akin to the brains of the operation, converting input from the remote into vital instructions for the motors. ESCs need to be incredibly robust and reliable, as they're responsible for critical functions like acceleration, braking, and control over uneven surfaces.

Over recent years, various manufacturers have devoted immense effort towards crafting intelligent ESCs. Some of the leading models now boast features like regenerative braking (which charges the battery when you brake), efficient heat management, sophisticated control algorithms for smoother rides, and even 'smart turn-on' features which power the skateboard as soon as it's kicked-off.

5.4. Board Design and Material Innovations

While the electric technology is exciting, the traditional skateboarding element must not be overlooked. The board's construction and design influence much more than aesthetics: they're crucial determinants of the ride's comfort, performance, and durability.

Classic wooden decks are still popular for their familiarity and flexibility, but innovative materials are increasingly gaining traction. Decks made from composite materials like carbon fiber and bamboo combine lightness with unprecedented durability and responsiveness. Meanwhile, innovative designs like drop-through decks and wider trucks are pushing the boundaries of what's possible in terms of control and stability.

5.5. The Lighter Side: LEDs and Underglow

While LED lighting might appear to be a purely aesthetic addition, it serves a critical functional purpose: safety. With the rise in popularity of night riding, visibility became paramount. Underglow LEDs not only accentuate the look of a moving board but also make night riders more visible to vehicles and pedestrians.

5.6. The Future: AI and Autonomous Features

Looking ahead, artificial intelligence (AI) and autonomous features may not be far-fetched for electric skateboards. Machine learning can be leveraged to adapt the ride to a user's habits over time, offering a more personalized experience. Predictive maintenance features could notify users about potential component failures before they even happen, based on extensive data analysis.

In conclusion, the world of electric skateboarding is in constant evolution, with continuous tech innovations offering fresh and thrilling ways to cruise through your city. Indeed, from massive leaps in power systems to exciting explorations into AI, it seems there's no slowing down this electrifying revolution in personal transport!

Chapter 6. Safety Measures: Gear, Tips, and Techniques

Before engaging with an electric skateboard, safety should be your primary concern. The thrill of breezing through city streets shouldn't sideline the necessity of understanding gear, techniques, and tips to remain safe while riding. This chapter will elaborate on vital safety measures, addressing them in a comprehensive manner.

6.1. Essential Safety Gear

The importance of wearing the right safety gear while using an electric skateboard cannot be stressed enough. Gear ensures you are best prepared to face any potential falls or collisions with minimum impact. Let's explore these safety instruments in detail.

1. Helmet: Arguably the most critical safety component, helmets help prevent serious head injuries. Choose one that comfortably fits your head and complies with safety standards. They can be full face or standard, depending on your preference and the kind of terrain you often ride on.

2. Knee and Elbow Pads: These pads provide cushioning to your joints, protecting them from scrapes or more serious injuries during a fall. Ensure they fit properly without restricting movement.

3. Wrist Guards: Wrist injuries are common with electric skateboarding. Wrist guards prevent your wrist from bearing the brunt of an impact during a fall, reducing injury risk.

4. Gloves: Gloves with wrist guards are even better as they also protect your hands from scrapes.

5. Body Armor: For more experienced riders who like to push the limits, body armor can provide an extra layer of protection.

6. Lights and Reflectors: Visibility is essential, especially while riding at night or in low-light conditions. Attach lights to your board or helmet and wear clothing with reflective elements to make sure you're seen.

6.2. Ride Safely: Tips and Strategies

Safety is as much about the right riding strategies as it is about gear. Here are a few pointers to keep in mind while riding.

1. Educate yourself: Before you start cruising, understand the anatomy of your board, its working principle, and how to handle it in various conditions.

2. Start slow: If you're new to electric skateboards, start on a flat, open surface and gradually increase your speed.

3. Positioning: Stand in the center of the board with feet shoulder-width apart, knees slightly bent and body leaning forward slightly. This provides balance.

4. Avoid distractions: Listening to music or texting while riding can lead to awareness lapses, increasing the risk of accidents. Always maintain complete focus on the road.

5. Don't push the limits: Every rider has a comfort zone. Don't try to ride beyond your skill level to avoid accidents.

6. Follow traffic rules: Always abide by local traffic laws just as any other vehicle would.

6.3. Protective Techniques

Understanding the dynamics of a fall helps to employ preventive action. Developing techniques to handle unexpected falls can lessen the chance of severe injury.

1. Learn to fall: Falling is inevitable, but how you fall can change

the outcome. Always aim to roll or slide during a fall, distributing the impact instead of concentrating it in one area.

2. Use your knees: Bend your knees and stay flexible. By keeping your center of gravity lower, you can maintain better control over your board.

3. Practice emergency stops: Develop the right skills to halt your board safely in emergencies.

4. Avoid locking your knees: You need a certain level of flexibility when riding, a stiffness in your legs can lead to unexpected tumbles.

5. Keep calm: Panic often leads to mistakes. Keeping calm helps manage unexpected issues on the board.

This chapter provides in-depth insights about safety gear, riding strategies, and protective techniques on an electric skateboard. It is not an exhaustive list; always keep learning and stay open to new tips and techniques as you progress on your electrifying journey.

Chapter 7. Choosing Your First Electric Skateboard: A Detailed Buying Guide

Getting started with the world of electric skateboarding can be a bit daunting with so many choices on offer. Never fear, though, this guide will walk you through the important factors to consider when buying your first e-skate.

7.1. Understanding Your Needs

Before you start looking for specific brands or models, first consider why you are in the market for an electric skateboard. Are you considering it for a commute to work or school, or perhaps for fun and leisure? Maybe you are a skateboarder looking to take your sport to the next level.

Each of these requirements might necessitate a different kind of electric skateboard. For instance, commuting users might prioritize range and portability, while those looking for leisure might focus on speed and maneuverability.

So, take a moment to identify and list down your needs as individual rider.

7.2. The Types of Electric Skateboards

Once you've determined your needs, it's time to learn about the different types of electric skateboards available in the market. There are primarily three types: shortboards, longboards, and all-terrain boards.

1. Shortboards: Generally measuring around 27 to 36 inches, these are compact and lightweight, making them perfect for quick commutes or trips. However, due to their size, they generally offer less stability, especially at higher speeds.

2. Longboards: These boards, generally measuring between 37 to 52 inches, are known for stability and are excellent for cruising or downhill riding. They often have larger batteries, providing longer range.

3. All-Terrain Boards: These are designed to handle multiple types of terrain, from smooth asphalt to rugged off-road trails. The large, wide wheels can roll over rocks and cracks with ease, but the size and weight make them less portable.

Evaluate the options and see which type of board fits your needs the best.

7.3. Key Factors to Consider

Now that you've worked out your needs and learned about the different types of electric skateboards, let's review the key factors to consider when choosing your first electric skateboard.

7.3.1. Range

Range refers to how far the skateboard can travel on a single charge. This can vary greatly depending on the type of skateboard and its battery capacity. If you plan to use the skateboard for commuting long distances, you probably need a long-range skateboard.

When checking the specifications, do note that the listed range is often tested under optimal conditions. Factors like the rider's weight, riding style, terrain inclines, and frequent starts and stops, can significantly reduce the actual range.

So, if your commute is 10 kilometers, consider a skateboard with at least twice that range to ensure you don't run out of battery mid-way.

7.3.2. Speed

Everyone loves a speedy ride, but as a beginner, it's crucial to find a safe and comfortable speed. The top speed offered by electric skateboards can vary wildly, from a conservative 10 mph to neck-breaking speeds upward of 25 mph or more.

If you're a beginner, it's good to start with slower speeds and gradually increase as you build confidence and proficiency. Look out for boards that offer multiple riding modes or speed settings, as they can help control your speed as you learn.

7.3.3. Weight

For situations where you'll have to carry your skateboard, such as indoor offices or public transportation, the weight of the skateboard can become crucial.

Longboards and all-terrain boards are usually heavier due to their size, additional battery capacity, and motor power. For an ultra-portable option, consider shortboards.

7.3.4. Motor Type: Hub vs Belt Driven

Electric skateboards are powered by either a hub or a belt-driven motor.

1. Hub Motors: These are built directly into the wheels of the skateboard. They are quieter, require less maintenance, and provide a more authentic skateboard feel. However, they might be less powerful and offer less torque than belt-driven systems.

2. Belt Driven Motors: The electric motor powers the wheels via a rubber belt. These systems offer higher torque (great for hill climbs), higher speeds, and better braking. However, they are

often louder, require more maintenance, and if the belt breaks, the board will be inoperable until it's replaced.

You will need to weigh these pros and cons to decide what suits you best.

7.3.5. Battery: Removable vs Non-removable

In addition to considering battery capacity (which dictates range), another important aspect to consider is whether the battery is removable.

A removable battery allows you to carry a spare and swap it when your charge runs low, effectively doubling your range. They are also useful if the battery fails or degrades over time; you can replace the battery rather than the entire skateboard.

Non-removable batteries, on the other hand, lead to less hassle as you won't have to carry an extra battery or worry about changing it.

7.3.6. Wheels

Different wheels are suited for different terrains.

Soft wheels are more suited for cruising on rough surfaces, giving a buttery smooth glide. They grip well but reduce speed and range.

Hard wheels are great for slides and more professional riding styles. They also improve speed and range compared to softer wheels, but they provide less grip and less smooth rides on rough surfaces.

Larger diameter wheels will cross over debris and cracks better than smaller wheels but come at the expense of acceleration as they require more torque to move.

7.3.7. Price

Finally, think about your budget. Electric skateboards vary greatly in price, from $200 to $2000 and more. Generally, inexpensive boards have less power, lower range, and are less durable. More expensive ones usually offer superior build quality, higher speeds, longer ranges, and additional neat features.

Remember, it's not just about finding the cheapest option, but getting value for your money.

7.4. Customer Reviews and Support

Before making your final decision, it's always wise to check out customer reviews for firsthand accounts of user experiences. Check for consistent praise or complaints about aspects like build quality, battery life, and customer service.

Also, consider post-purchase support. If something goes wrong with your board, does the company offer quick and helpful customer service? Do they provide spare parts for sale? In the unlikely event that you encounter a problem with your electric skateboard, these considerations could make a big difference.

7.5. Conclusion

Choosing your first electric skateboard is an exciting experience. As you make this decision, remember to prioritize safety alongside performance. Always wear a helmet, and even consider elbow and knee protectors until you gain confidence and skill in your new sport.

Remember, this guide is just the starting point! Always be curious and keep learning as you cruise through the thrilling world of electric skateboarding!

Chapter 8. Maintenance and Upgrades: Keeping Your Ride in Top Shape

Maintaining an electric skateboard not only prolongs its life but also ensures a safe and enjoyable ride every time. In this section, you'll learn everything from the basics of routine maintenance, to troubleshooting common issues, and making upgrades to fine-tune your performance or accommodate your changing needs.

Moreover, understanding your board's components can help you make informed decisions when shopping for replacements or upgrades. You should pay close attention to your board's deck, motors, wheels, trucks, bearings, and battery. In the following sections, we'll look at each element, its maintenance procedures, and upgrade options.

8.1. Understanding Your Electric Skateboard

Before you can perform maintenance or seek upgrades, you need to understand your board's components. Make no mistake - the world of electric skateboarding is filled with a wide range of product variety and technical specifications.

An electric skateboard typically consists of a deck, motors, wheels, trucks, bearings, bushings, and a battery compartment. These fundamental components, while similar to regular skateboards, come with their unique maintenance needs due to the electrical and mechanical systems.

We'll delve into each of these components, providing insights into their functions, troubleshooting steps, and potential upgrades to enhance your ride.

8.2. Deck Maintenance and Upgrade Options

The deck of your skateboard is more than just a platform for your feet. It provides key structural integrity and affects ride comfort and control.

To maintain your deck, regularly check for signs of wear such as cracks or splits, especially after heavy use. Clean your deck with mild soap and water, avoiding the electrical components. If your grip tape, the rough layer on top of the deck providing foot traction, becomes dirty or worn out, replace it to maintain control.

Upgrades for deck mostly come down to personal preference and riding style. Some prefer flexible decks for their shock-absorbing qualities while others prefer stiffer decks for stability at high speeds. Consider materials (such as bamboo for flexibility or maple for rigidity), deck length, and concave shape when looking for upgrades.

8.3. Caring for Your Motors

The motors on an e-board demand much attention. Brushless motors - the most commonly used due to their efficiency and longevity - still need regular inspections to ensure smooth operation. Check for loose connections and signs of physical damage. Listen for any abnormal noises during operation that may indicate issues with motor windings or bearings.

Motor upgrades can provide higher top speeds or greater torque for uphill climbs. However, you need to ensure compatibility with your batteries and speed controllers, keeping in mind that more powerful motors may demand more battery life.

8.4. Wheel Maintenance and Replacement

Wheels will wear down over time, affecting ride quality and control. Regularly inspect them for cracks or chunking and ensure they spin freely without wobbling.

Upgrading wheels can significantly influence your ride. Larger wheels can handle rough terrain better but may decrease acceleration, while smaller wheels offer improved acceleration but a bumpier ride. The hardness or softness of the wheel also impacts grip and ride feel.

8.5. Maintaining Trucks and Bushings

Trucks connect the wheels to the deck and allow turning and carving, while bushings affect how trucks respond to rider weight shifts. Regularly clean your trucks, check for physical damage, and replace any bushings that start feeling too loose or tight. If the board veers to one side during a ride, it's a sign of truck misalignment that needs adjustment.

The right truck and bushing upgrades will depend on your riding style. For instance, wider trucks can add stability but may reduce maneuverability. Bushing durometer (hardness) and shape dramatically impact turning responsiveness.

8.6. Bearings and Their Role

Bearings enable smooth wheel movement. Clean and lubricate bearings every few weeks, and replace them if they make grinding noises or cause wheels to spin unevenly.

When it's time for an upgrade, look for high-quality bearings that promise less rolling resistance. Ceramic bearings, for instance, are a popular choice due to their heat- and corrosion-resistant properties.

8.7. Battery Care and Upgrades

The battery is the lifeblood of an electric skateboard, and proper care helps extend its lifespan. Always follow the manufacturer's specific charging instructions, avoid deep discharges, and store the battery properly in a cool, dry place.

Considering an upgrade? A higher-capacity battery can increase your range, but also ensure compatibility with your skateboard's other components. Lithium-ion batteries are a popular choice due to their high energy density and long lifecycles.

In conclusion, maintaining and upgrading an electric skateboard isn't just about ensuring high performance or extending lifespan. It helps deliver a safer, more enjoyable ride, while allowing you to customize your board according to your evolving needs. With the right knowledge and equipment at your disposal, you can truly shape the future of your electric skateboarding experience.

NOTE Always ensure that maintenance and upgrades adhere to your product's warranty terms and safety guidelines. We recommend seeking professional help for complex issues or upgrades to ensure safety and reliability.

Chapter 9. Maximizing Battery Life: Tips and Tricks

As electric skateboards become more prevalent in our streets and parks, understanding the nuances of their operation becomes vital. Among the components that make up an electric skateboard, the battery plays an essential role as it powers the board and enables its operation. Maximizing its life becomes crucial to ensure a longer run time, a greater lifespan for the board, and, most importantly, a better riding experience.

9.1. Understanding Battery Basics

An electric skateboard's battery is essentially an energy storage unit that powers the electric motor, ultimately propelling the board. Most electric skateboards use lithium-ion batteries due to their excellent energy-to-weight ratios, a pivotal feature when considering the need for lightness and portability.

Battery life is conventionally measured in cycles, which represents the number of full charges and discharges the battery can handle before its potential starts to significantly deteriorate. Interestingly, battery life also depends on the way the battery is used and maintained.

Here are some general rules to understand:

- The faster you drain a battery, the shorter its lifespan.

- Regular and complete charging-discharging cycles help to ensure optimal battery health.

- Overcharging or discharging the batteries excessively can damage them and reduce their lifespans.

By keeping these rules in mind and making suitable adjustments in usage patterns, it's possible to make giant leaps in the longevity of your electric skateboard's batteries.

9.2. Battery Maintenance Tips

Proper maintenance begins with understanding your battery's needs. Here are some actionable tips to extend your battery's life:

1. Use an appropriate charger: Always use the charger supplied by the manufacturer. These are designed to match the specific voltage and amperage requirements of your battery, ensuring safe and efficient charging.

2. Never overcharge: As mentioned before, overcharging can severely degrade your battery life over time. Using a smart charger, which automatically cuts off power when the battery is fully charged, can prevent overcharging.

3. Avoid complete discharges: Allow your battery to discharge only up to 20%. Nothing kills a battery faster than complete discharges.

4. Proper storage: If you don't plan to use your skateboard for a long time, store the battery at a half-charge in a cool, dry place to keep it healthy.

9.3. Influence of Riding Habits

Your riding habits significantly influence your skateboard's battery life. Understand and adapt your usage patterns to amplify battery performance:

1. Ride smoothly: Hard acceleration and rapid deceleration are not your battery's best friends. Smooth, gradual movements help extend battery life.

2. Be mindful of the terrain: Smooth, flat surfaces are ideal for electric skateboards. Riding on rough terrains or steep inclines can drain the battery faster.

3. Minimize weight: The heavier your board, the more the battery has to work. Try to lessen any unnecessary weight for the best battery performance.

4. Manage your speed: Higher speeds can quickly deplete your battery. Maintain moderate speeds to achieve a balance between performance and battery consumption.

9.4. Weather Impacts on Battery Life

Outside environmental conditions directly affect battery performance. Extreme temperatures on either side of the scale are harmful. Batteries perform at their best in average room-temperature conditions.

Skateboarding during very hot or cold weather is not recommended due to the potential toll on the battery's lifecycle. Especially, avoid charging a battery that's still hot from usage or one that's notably cold. Allow the battery to reach room temperature before recharging.

9.5. Regular Check-ups and Replacements

Even with perfect maintenance, batteries degrade over time, reducing their performance. Regular check-ups help to understand the battery's health and, if necessary, signalling when it's time for a replacement. Check for visible deformities, unusually long charging times, or reduced usage times - these are signs it may be time to replace your battery.

Though advanced batteries are in development, for now, we must make the best of what we have at our disposal. By following the tips and tricks laid out in this chapter, you can ensure that you are riding your electric skateboard in the most efficient way possible, maximizing the life and performance of your battery, and ultimately your enjoyment of this remarkable ride.

Chapter 10. The Future of Electric Skateboarding: Trends and Predictions

Even as we stand at the brink of an era aligned with electric mobility, it's crucial to gaze forward to see where the electric skateboard niche is headed. Trends and predictions can anticipate the trajectory of this sector, informing our understanding of the terrain we're yet to traverse. In the following discourse, we'll delve into the various factors shaping the industry — spanning technological advancements, regulatory hurdles, and consumer preferences.

10.1. Technological Advancements

The driving force behind the proliferation of electric skateboards is, without a doubt, the nuanced exploration of technology. We're experiencing significant developments in almost every aspect of these electric-powered devices.

1. **Better Battery Technologies:** Battery life has been a perennial challenge for electric skateboard manufacturers. However, the gradual transition from traditional Lithium-ion to Lithium-polymer batteries is promising longer range. Even more intriguing is the research into solid-state batteries, which would provide more power, longer life, and enhanced safety measures.

2. **Improved Motor Efficiency:** The quest for more powerful yet smaller and lighter motors is ongoing. The brushless DC motors (BLDC), characterized by low noise, high efficiency, and long lifespan, are already predominantly employed in electric skateboards. However, direct drive motors are gaining momentum, as they require fewer moving parts, offering a smoother ride with less maintenance required.

3. **Evolution of Smart Features:** With an influx of AI and IoT capabilities, electric skateboards are becoming smarter. Boards integrated with gyro sensors can help maintain balance while riding and are particularly useful for beginners. GPS-enabled boards offer riders the ability to track routes, distances, and speeds, providing valuable insights into their rides.

4. **Advances in Material Science:** Contemporary designs are focusing on lighter yet stronger materials. Integration of carbon fiber, a material known for its high stiffness, high tensile strength, low weight, and high-temperature tolerance, can lead to boards that are both high-performing and long-lasting.

10.2. Regulatory Challenges

While tech advancements are propelling the industry into the future, regulations can either accelerate or hinder its pace. Varied interpretations and inconsistencies in enforcing laws pertaining to electric skateboards can pose significant obstacles.

1. **Permitting Issues:** While some U.S. states and many European countries consider electric skateboards as 'Personal Light Electric Vehicles', others do not permit their use in public spaces at all. This legal ambiguity is likely to keep playing a significant role in shaping the growth of electric skateboarding.

2. **Helmet Mandates:** There is no clear consensus on helmet laws applicable to electric skateboard riders. Some regions require helmets for all ages, others for minors only, and some don't impose this rule at all. It's anticipated that mandatory helmet laws could become more prevalent to increase rider safety.

3. **Speed Limits:** The stipulated speed limit for electric skateboards varies greatly by location, with considerable discrepancies. A gradual standardization of these limits could provide a more predictable and safe riding experience, but it remains to be seen how this will evolve.

10.3. Consumer Trends

Finally, scrutinizing current user behaviors can offer clues into the future of the industry. There are key trends to note:

1. **Urban Commuting:** As urbanization continues unabated, and the need for quick, convenient, and eco-friendly commuting rises, electric skateboards are increasingly seen as a viable alternative to traditional transportation means.

2. **Recreational Use:** There's mounting interest in e-skateboarding as a hobby for thrill-seekers, especially among teens and young adults. This trend is expected to endure, fuelling demand for more advanced, sport-oriented boards.

3. **Demand for Customization:** Riders are seeking ways to customize their boards to suit their style and needs. This is leading to an upsurge in the aftermarket accessories sector, likely driving innovation and diversity in skateboard design and functionality.

To wrap up, the electric skateboard landscape is constantly shifting. It's a thrilling ride on a board that's being continually redefined by tech advancements, regulation changes, and evolving consumer preferences. The journey ahead promises more power, higher speeds, smart features, and sleek designs. As we push forward, we carry the hope of a future where electric skateboards are not just recreational toys but integral parts of our daily commute — embodying our strides towards sustainable mobility.

Chapter 11. The Community and Culture: Electric Skateboarding Around the World

The global acceptance and adoption of electric skateboarding have created vibrant cultures and communities worldwide, notably in countries like the United States, Australia, the United Kingdom, and several parts of Asia. This chapter delves into the unique vibes and characteristics of these trend-setting communities.

11.1. Understanding the Skateboarding Community Culture

A skateboard offers more than just a means of transport; it has long been a signal of a certain hip cultural identity. However, the introduction of electric skateboarding has stirred up the scene, culminating in a powerful intersection between traditional skateboard culture, tech enthusiasts, and city commuters seeking alternatives to conventional methods of transport. This hybrid culture champions values of innovation, respect for the environment, and a shared sense of community.

Electric skateboarding forums, clubs, and online groups have seen tremendous growth in recent years. Platforms like Reddit and Facebook harbor vibrant e-skate communities where members can share experiences, offer advice, and organize group rides. Moreover, websites such as Electric Skateboard HQ, esk8.news, and others serve as rich information hubs for both experienced and newbie riders.

11.2. The Growth and Influence of E-Skating Globally

In the USA, the electric skateboard revolution initially started among tech hobbyists. Silicon Valley engineers and developers began creating DIY e-board prototypes to solve the 'last mile' problem. Today, e-skating isn't just a geek delicacy anymore; it's become mainstream in many U.S. cities, impressively weaving convenience with adventure.

In Australia and the United Kingdom, the movement saw a different beginning. Most enthusiasts got into electric skateboarding because of the environmental benefits, replacing their fuel-guzzling vehicles with more sustainable, fun alternatives. Legislation in these regions tends to be e-skate friendly, thereby fostering its popularity.

Asia, particularly China, has been instrumental in the electric skating movement, not merely as a consumer base but through manufacturing power. Chinese enterprises like Meepo, Wowgo, and Backfire have dominated the mid-market segment of the e-skate industry, producing quality boards with competitive pricing.

11.3. Local Meetups and Events: A Place for Everything E-Skate

Community meetups, local rides, and competitions are fundamental aspects of the global e-skate culture. They represent opportunities for hobbyists, pros, and newcomers alike to connect, learn, and celebrate the electric revolution.

USA: The USA boasts of several electric skateboard conventions, races, and meetups every year. Events like the NYC Eboarding Collective and the Bay Area Esk8 group in California offer everyone—from seasoned pros to total newbies—a chance to participate.

Australia: Australia's Gold Coast and Sydney are home to some of the most active e-skating communities in the world. Organizations like ESK8 Brisbane arrange regular group rides, attracting hundreds of e-skaters from around the nation.

Europe: The UK and many other European countries have their own set of ride groups. In France, ESK8FR holds frequent meetup rides through picturesque Parisian streets, while the London E-Boarding Crew regularly meets for electric adventures across the British capital.

Asia: Meepo Board, a Chinese e-skate company, hosts frequent meetups, where everyone from enthusiasts to amateurs can attend, test out products, and join group rides.

11.4. Virtual Communities: Stay Connected, Anywhere, Anytime

With the internet becoming a primary mode of connection, e-skating communities have begun to thrive online as well. Reddit's r/ElectricSkateboarding community is a treasure trove of information and discussion, boasting members from all over the globe. Meanwhile, the Electric Skateboarding Discord Server offers real-time chat features, providing dynamic, immediate conversation for passionate e-skaters worldwide.

11.5. Holding Manufacturers Accountable: The Community's Role

Communities aren't just about celebrating the joys of electric skateboarding; they also play a crucial role in ensuring the industry advances responsibly. Members often come together to hold manufacturers accountable—for example, standing against companies that make false speed or range claims. Some even use social media platforms to encourage these manufacturers to improve warranty conditions, after-sales service, or customer support.

11.6. Conclusion: Towards a Sustainable Future

The electric skateboarding revolution is a testament to society's pivotal shift towards more sustainable forms of personal transport. The sense of community that this movement has cultivated across the globe speaks volumes about shared values and the collective direction of forward-thinking societies. As individuals come together to redefine what modern-day personal commute means, the world as a whole benefits.

This chapter's insights bear witness to the electric skateboard culture's global resonance, propelled by collective passion, innovation, and widespread commitment to a greener future. Through understanding these dynamics, we can better appreciate and engage with the world of electric skateboarding and contribute to its continued evolution.